Lullabies & Bedtime Stories

The Life, Times, & Music™ Series

Lullabies & Bedtime Stories

The Life, Times, & Music™ Series

Carin Dewhirst

Illustrations by Betsy Day

Friedman/Fairfax
Publishers

Dedication

**For Amanda Kate Lockwood and Hannah Claire Ramel,
who arrived just in time for lullabies.**

A FRIEDMAN GROUP BOOK

© 1994 by Michael Friedman Publishing Group, Inc.
Illustrations © 1994 by Betsy Day

ISBN 1-56799-086-X

THE LIFE, TIMES, & MUSIC ™ SERIES: LULLABIES & BEDTIME STORIES
was prepared and produced by
Michael Friedman Publishing Group, Inc.
15 West 26th Street
New York, New York 10010

Editor: Nathaniel Marunas
Art Director: Jeff Batzli
Designer: Tanya Ross-Hughes

Grateful acknowledgment is given to authors and publishers for permission to reprint material. In the case of any omissions, the publishers will be pleased to make suitable acknowledgments in future editions.

Printed in the United States of America

For bulk purchases and special sales, please contact:
Friedman/Fairfax Publishers
Attention: Sales Department
15 West 26 Street
New York, NY 10010
(212) 685-6610 FAX (212) 685-1307

Contents

Introduction

Removing the dread from bedtime is a

challenge for parents everywhere. The

following recipe is recommended as a

means to coax even the most reluctant child

to fall asleep. Combine the ingredients in

the order listed and prepare for a deep

and restful sleep. Sweet dreams!

One warm bath, preferably with bubbles

One comfortable bed, definitely with snuggles

One story, interesting and amusing

One lullaby, soft and soothing.

Bedtime, Night Rhyme

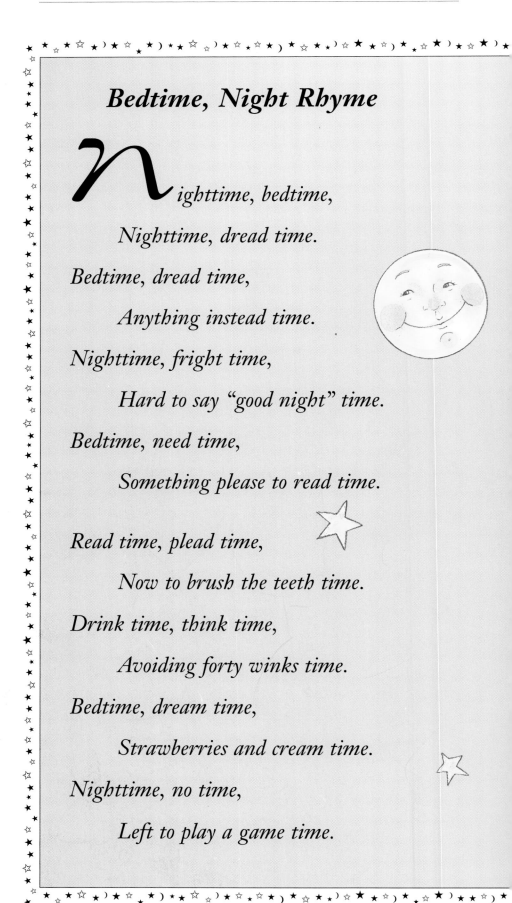

Nighttime, bedtime,

Nighttime, dread time.

Bedtime, dread time,

Anything instead time.

Nighttime, fright time,

Hard to say "good night" time.

Bedtime, need time,

Something please to read time.

Read time, plead time,

Now to brush the teeth time.

Drink time, think time,

Avoiding forty winks time.

Bedtime, dream time,

Strawberries and cream time.

Nighttime, no time,

Left to play a game time.

Bedtime, nighttime,

Bedtime, right time,

Why time, cry time,

Sing a lullaby time.

Bedtime, stall time,

Say "good night" to all time.

Bedtime, it's time

At the end of this rhyme.

—Joan Dewhirst

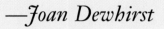

Lullaby

For centuries the soothing strains of lullabies have helped countless numbers of restless children to fall asleep. The earliest lullabies had no words; instead, they were melodies that were hummed or crooned using syllables that made no sense, but produced soothing, lulling sounds. Some of these nonsense sounds, such as "loo-loo," "la-la," and "lullay," are refrains in popular lullabies even today.

The word *lullaby* may actually be a contraction of *lulla,* from the ancient Norse (also note *lulla* in Swedish, *lulle* in Danish), meaning "to calm with gentle sounds," and *baby.* In Italy a lullaby is called *ninna nanna*; in France, *berceuse*; and in Germany, *Wiegenlied.* In English it is a "cradlesong."

Lullabies are part of the private language that a loving parent uses to commune with his or her baby. In this warm and intimate secret language, words that calm fears and dry tears, comfort, soothe, reassure, and amuse help children drift into the world of sleep. Often described as the "Land of Nod," sleep has been personified in the form of angels, fairy godmothers, the Sandman (who distributes "sleep dust"), and even a small child called Willie Winkie:

> **Wee Willie Winkie runs through the town,**
>
> **Upstairs and downstairs in his nightgown,**
>
> **Rapping at the window, crying through the lock;**
>
> **"Are all the children in their beds,**
>
> **It's past eight o'clock!**

A welcome part of falling asleep is the anticipation of dreaming. Many lullabies close with the words, "Goodnight, sweet dreams." Frederica von Stade hopes that her child will "sleep with a sweet dream." It is a fact that everyone—from little babies to people in their nineties—dreams. Most dreams are forgotten, but sometimes one of these nighttime visions will be vividly remembered, as if it had actually happened.

Bedtime Round/City Lullaby

This song by Tom Chapin has two parts. The first part, "Bedtime Round," is about trying to put off going to bed by asking for every little thing you can think of, until suddenly...you fall asleep.

A "round" is a special kind of song that features different voices, beginning at slightly different times, singing the same melody.

Listen to the three voices in the songs as they sing the words, "Mom, I need another story...just a short one/Mom, I need another glass of water...just a small one/Mom, I need another hug." Saying goodbye to the activities of daytime and hello to the quiet darkness of nighttime can be difficult. Sometimes all you really need is another hug.

The second part of the song, "City Lullaby," is about going to sleep in a busy city. Falling asleep sounds so easy, but what if you live in a place like New York City or San Francisco, cities that stay awake all night? Well, if you're tired enough, the sounds of sirens and car horns, clocks ticking and telephones ringing, and screeching brakes soon become melodic murmurs that rhythmically lull you to sleep.

Time for Bed

It's time for bed

Time to say good night now

So snuggle up and turn out the light now

Time to say so long to the day

Start your snorin'

Snoozin' the night away.

—T. Guernsey and Rory

When it's time for bed it's also time for bedtime stories. This story is about Small Bear, who wanted very much to know why she had to go to bed.

"Why do I have to go to bed?" Small Bear asked her parents one evening.

"Well," said her mother, "you have to go to bed because it is bedtime."

"But why is now bedtime? Why not later?"

"Well," said her father, "you are a very small bear and now is the bedtime for very small bears."

"But why do I have to go to bed at all?"

"Well," said her mother, "the bodies of very small bears tire easily and need plenty of rest to become very big bears."

"But my body isn't tired at all," Small Bear responded. And with that she jumped out of bed and ran around the room. She shouted, "See, I'm not sleepy at all!" and raced around the room again. "Why do I have to go to bed?" Small Bear hollered.

Small Bear's parents looked at each other and yawned. "Well," Small Bear's father said, "perhaps some

of the very wise animals of the forest will have your answer. We will go and ask them."

Small Bear was very glad to be out on a nighttime walk after her bedtime. She practically raced down the moonlit path into the woods. Her parents followed a few steps behind. Soon they came to a tall, tall tree with a small red door. This was the door to Squirrel's tree house. Small Bear stood on her tiptoes to reach the acorn-shaped door knocker, and she rapped it three times.

She heard tip-tapping sounds coming from high in the tree as Squirrel walked down the many wooden steps from his family's cozy quarters in the treetop. Squirrel finally came to the door and opened it. He looked down at Small Bear and blinked several times.

Small Bear spoke politely, "My parents sent me to ask you why I have to go to bed. Do you know why?"

Squirrel looked at the very wide-awake little bear and blinked a few times more. He was having trouble keeping his eyes open. He started to speak, but he was caught by a long, wide yawn. "So sorry, Small Bear," he said. "I do know the answerrrr..." he yawned again, "but I am too tired to tell you right now. Go ask Otter, perhaps she can help you."

Small Bear thanked Squirrel kindly, then turned down the path with her parents. When they heard the rushing river, they knew they were near the home of Otter. A group of large, smooth boulders marked the spot. Small Bear tossed three pebbles lightly into the river with a plunk, shplunk, kerplunk. Soon Otter came to the suface, slithered onto a rock, and rubbed her eyes with her paws.

"Oh, Otter, my parents and Squirrel sent me to ask you why I have to go to bed. Do you know why?" Small Bear inquired.

"Well, of course I do," Otter said quickly. "But I was just about to go to bed myself. I am too sleepy to tell you just now. Go ask Bird. I'm sure he knows the answer. I am off to bed right now!"

And Otter slipped silently back into the river.

As Otter swam away, Small Bear thanked her kindly and went on down the path with her parents. They didn't walk quite as fast as before. After a short distance, Small Bear asked if she could ride on her mother's back. Small Bear said she wanted to be up high so she could see better, but her father thought she looked a little sleepy. Farther on they came to the old oak where Bird lived. From one branch a long leafy vine dangled almost to the ground. This was Bird's doorbell. Small

Bear pulled it three times. They heard a faint ringing in the treetops, and soon Bird fluttered down to greet them. He perched himself on Small Bear's paw. "Hello, friends," he chirped.

"Oh, Bird," Small Bear said, "my parents, Squirrel, and Otter sent me to ask you why I have to go to bed. Tell me, do you know the reason?"

Bird turned his head to one side and then the other to get a good look at Small Bear. "It is funny that you should ask, for I was just singing my babies a lullaby. It made me so sleepy I decided to go to bed myself. I do know the answer, but I am too tired to tell you now. Go ask Deer. She knows everything." With a wave, Bird took off for his bed in the treetop.

Small Bear thanked Bird kindly, and the Bear family went on down the path deeper into the wood. Small Bear's father carried her in his arms. In a short while they came to a clearing surrounded by ferns. This was where Deer lived with her fawn. Small Bear hardly lifted her head from her father's shoulder as they approached Deer. In a sleepy voice Small Bear said to Deer, "My parents, Squirrel, Otter, and Bird sent me to ask you why I have to go to bed. But I am too tired to listen to your answer right now." And with that Small Bear snuggled against her father's shoulder and fell fast asleep.

Deer looked at Small Bear and her parents. Her warm, kind eyes glistened in the moonlight. Then she said quietly, "Goodnight, Small Bear, sweet dreams."

Baby of Mine

Lullabies have been described as heart-songs or litanies of love—songs of intimacy with lyrics that literally plumb the depths of a parent's love for his or her child. As Deniece Williams softly confesses in her tender song,

I'll hold you close, baby of mine,

Rocking you gently is simply a joy;

Baby of mine, I love you so

I can't resist giving you kisses galore.

Lullabies such as this confirm the safety and security of parental love and can be instrumental in establishing very special bonds between parent and child. They are songs filled with joy and contentment, sung solely for the child but meant for anyone to hear. They are examples of a technique that is known as "singing outward."

In contrast are those lullabies meant to be sung to a child in strictest privacy. During these private moments the fretful baby becomes an uncomprehending confidant as its mother confesses her innermost thoughts. Consider this Portuguese lullaby:

Whoever has little children

Must sing to them;

But how often, instead of singing,

We feel like crying.

Or this one from Germany:

> **Sleep while I'm brushing the flies from your brow;**
>
> **This is the time, love, to sleep and to play.**
>
> **Later, oh later is not like today;**
>
> **When care and trouble and sorrow come sore,**
>
> **You never will sleep, love, as sound as before.**

Often the lyrics become a mother's lament, expressing regrets at being housebound and overburdened with work, or concern that there might not be enough food for the family to eat. Known as "singing inward," these lullabies serve a twofold purpose: the baby is lulled to sleep and the mother is able to vent her frustrations and emotions privately.

Lullabies have also been known to put parents to sleep, sometimes before their children. This Italian lullaby relates:

> **Rock-a-bye, rock-a-bye;**
>
> **The child puts mother to sleep;**
>
> **And mother shall sleep**
>
> **If baby will sleep.**

Innocent One

Have you ever wondered what makes lullabies work? What secret ingredient is in these quiet melodies that causes a person to fall asleep? The power lies in the rhythm, a steady tick-tock beat (much like that of a metronome or pendulum) that has a hypnotic ability to produce sleep. The soothing

quality of such a rhythm may be linked to the fact that one of the first sensations a baby experiences—even before birth—is the regular beat of its mother's heart.

See for yourself. Put on your pajamas, snuggle up in bed, close your eyes, and listen closely as Chris Spheeris performs "Innocent One." The recording begins with the sounds of a music box being wound up and a baby's soft gurgling noises. Then the volume increases and the melody unfolds, but the rhythm remains constant. You can feel yourself caught up in the steady, almost rocking movement as the music swells and swells. Then, gradually, ever so slightly, the tune softens, slows, and finally stops. Watch out—the magic of this lullaby is powerful. Sleep well.

Close Your Eyes

There's a long, long trail a-winding

Into the land of my dreams,

Where the nightingales are singing

And a white moon beams.

—Stoddard King

Where do you go when you dream? In the song "Close Your Eyes" by Priscilla Herdman, dreamland is described as "a bright enchanted land where the unicorn dances," but your own dreamland can be whatever you want it to be. There once was a toy rocking horse that would gallop away to its own dreamland, where rocking horses play. Close your eyes and listen to the story of this enchanted land.

Very long ago, in the time of castles, dragons, and fairy godmothers, there was a magical rocking horse named Roland. A little Prince got Roland on his fifth birthday— the rocking horse was a present from the Prince's fairy godmother. Roland was a champion rocking horse. He stood about eight hands high, and his mane, tail, and coat were glossy black. Strapped on his back was a red and tan leather saddle with fancy golden stirrups. Tiny brass bells hung from his braided silk bridle and reins, jingling whenever he rocked to-and-fro.

When the Prince rode Roland, he imagined he was The Knight of All Knights. He and Roland rode fast and sure through perilous forests. They battled dangerous foes and rescued people who were in trouble. The Prince played with Roland all day long, then placed him in his own little stall made of painted wood. There Roland ate his oats (actually they were small painted beads) out of a toy bucket.

One night the Prince thought he heard whinnying from Roland's little stall. He went to Roland and saw big tears coming from the horse's glass eyes. The Prince was so moved he began to weep himself. He touched Roland's wet cheek and asked him what was wrong.

"I want to go to my home," Roland neighed, "beyond the mists of the sea and over the mountain peaks. I want to go to Rocking Horse Land."

The Prince hugged Roland and said, "I want you to be happy, but I want you to be here for me to play with. Will you stay in Rocking Horse Land forever?"

"I will come back whenever you wish me to. Take a bell from my reins. Ring it, wish for me, and I will return."

With that the Prince opened his bedroom window so that Roland could leave. The rocking horse rocked back and forth, back and forth until his rockers disappeared. Then Roland galloped out the window off beyond the mists of the sea and over the mountain peaks.

The next morning the Prince missed Roland. He rang the bell, wished hard, and the rocking horse magically appeared. They played together till the sun set, then the Prince opened his window and Roland went off to Rocking Horse Land.

Every day the two friends played together, until the Prince's sixth birthday. On this day Roland came as usual to play, but very soon after the Prince became distracted. His father, the King, had given him a real live horse, and the Prince soon forgot all about Roland. The rocking horse stood alone, trapped in his wooden stall with his toy bucket of oats, waiting for the Prince and dreaming of Rocking Horse Land.

Many weeks later, while the Prince was out riding his real horse, he reached into his pocket and felt the tiny brass bell. Love and sadness filled his heart. The Prince returned to the castle, went to Roland's stall, and knelt by his once-favorite toy.

"Oh, Roland, I am so sorry," he cried. "You can go now to Rocking Horse Land where you will be happy." The Prince opened the window and watched Roland gallop away beyond the mists of the sea and over the mountain peaks. The Prince silently wished Roland well, but he knew that he would never wish for his friend to return.

The Prince walked up into the tallest tower in the castle, the one that looked out over the sea. He leaned out a window and tossed the tiny brass bell into the churning, frothy water. He had neglected Roland and he was sorry. He wanted the rocking horse to be happy so he let him go forever.

Years and years went by and the Prince grew up. He became King himself and had a son who was Prince. On the morning of this little Prince's fifth birthday, the King came to his son's room with birthday greetings.

The King found the little Prince playing boisterously on a toy rocking horse. "Oh, Father," the little Prince yelled with glee, "look at my wonderful toy! What shall I call him?" The King looked fondly at the rocking horse with its glossy black coat and familiar red and tan saddle with fancy golden stirrups. He said, "Call him Roland." And the little Prince did.

Night Song

*Night comes and covers all
the sky
With a quilt of stars and the moon
on high.
The air is soft as a lullaby
All is still...hush!*

Daylight is gone, no more to play

Until tomorrow's dawning ray.

Peace and quiet have come to stay

All is still...hush!

Beds are open, smooth and deep

Cuddly toys are there to keep

Dreamers safe while fast

asleep.

All is still...hush!

—Joan Dewhirst

Too-Ra-Loo-Ra-Loo-Ral

There is a lullaby that's just right for everyone because lullabies come in many varieties. "Too-Ra-Loo-Ra-Loo-Ral (That's an Irish Lullaby)" is a special kind of lullaby that uses sounds that are soothing to the ear. Some believe that lullabies help people sleep because of the hypnotic combination of the vibrations of the voice and the song's rhythm.

Some of the most soothing lullabies have no real words at all. Instead, these lullabies have nonsense sounds that are sung to a beat that mimics the to-and-fro motion of a cradle or rocking chair. In fact, that *one-and-two-and-one-and-two-and* rhythm seems to make people sleepy all over the world, no matter what words or sounds are sung to it. In English-speaking countries, the sounds *ba-ah ba-ah* are popular lullaby sounds, while *aah-aah aah-aah* are the traditional sounds in Asian and Spanish lullabies. In ancient Rome over one thousand years ago, nurses hummed the sound *lalla* over and over again to help infants go to sleep. No one really knows what *lalla* means, although it sounds like an even older Greek word for the sound of the sea murmuring on the beach.

In some lullabies, of course, the words are very important. For instance, many lullabies promise gifts to a child in return for the child's good behavior. Some of these gifts are simple, like the one in "Bye, Baby Bunting," a Mother Goose rhyme that is often sung as a lullaby (the word *bunting* is an old term of endearment that means "short and thick...as a plump child"):

Bye, Baby Bunting, your daddie's gone a hunting,

Gone to get a little rabbit-skin

To wrap a Baby Bunting in.

Other lullabies, such as this one from Norway, promise children tasty things to eat (in days gone by *thou* and *thee* were words for "you"):

If thou will but sleep and mind me,

Then a sweet cake I will find thee.

Have you ever been promised the moon and the stars? There are some lullabies that playfully promise gifts that are impossible to give. This old North American folk lullaby is a good example:

Lu la lu la lu la lu la by by,

Didja want the moon to play with

Or the stars to run away with?

They'll come if you don't cry.

If presents don't work, sometimes a lullaby will threaten
the fussy child with a gentle punishment. This little German
song is typical:

Sleep, baby, sleep, I can see two little sheep;

One is black and one is white,

And if you do not sleep tonight,

First the black and then the white

Will give your toes a little bite.

To the reader: Try making up your own tune to go along with these words (don't forget to lightly bite or pinch the toes of the child you are singing to).

If you prefer to make up words to a melody you already know, try altering the lyrics to the classic lullaby "Hush, Little Baby." Think of your child's favorite things and use them in place of the "mockingbird," "diamond ring," and so forth. You can create entirely new rhymes to complete the verses:

Hush, little baby, doncha make a peep,

'Cause mama's gonna buy you a fancy jeep.

And if that jeep runs out of gas,

Mama's gonna buy you a boat and mast.

If you sail the ocean deep,

Soon you will be fast asleep.

Pet Names

*B*abies have names that are just
their own,
But pet names abound all over the globe.

In English it's honeybunch, lambkin,
and angel,
While Syrian babies are pretty as basil.

Parents in Sicily wish bunches of jasmine
goodnight,
In Persia babes are tulips and in China
lily-whites.

In India a baby is pretty as a lotus,
And Irish babes are poppets or precious.

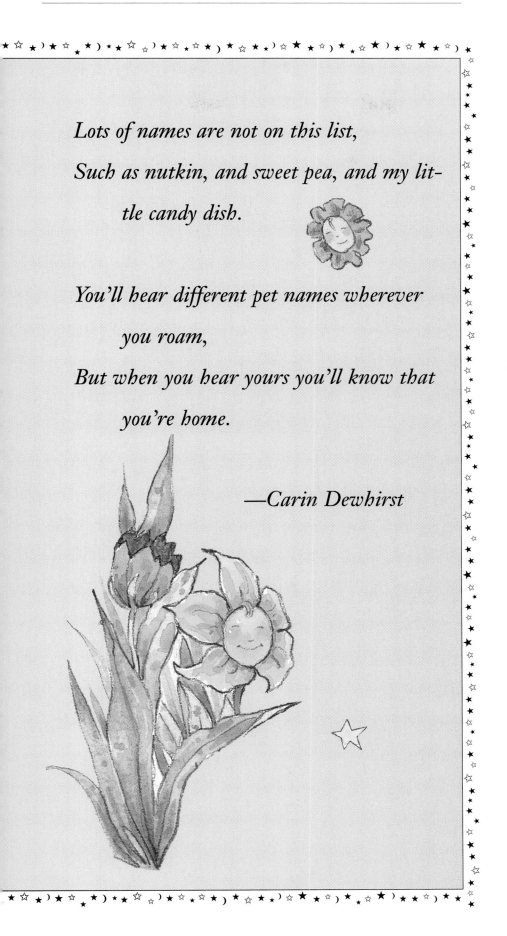

Lots of names are not on this list,

Such as nutkin, and sweet pea, and my lit-

tle candy dish.

You'll hear different pet names wherever

you roam,

But when you hear yours you'll know that

you're home.

—Carin Dewhirst

Sweet and Low

In many lullabies a child is described as something other than just a child. He or she is transformed by the singer into "sweet darling," "lovely one," or "perfect one." In the song "Sweet and Low," the little baby is "my little one" and "my pretty one." These special names are called terms of endearment, "little" names, or "pet" names. What are your pet names?

If apples were pears,

And peaches were plums,

And the rose had a different name—

If tigers were bears,

And fingers were thumbs,

I'd love you just the same.

— anonymous

In many places children are compared with beautiful flowers. Jasmine flowers have a lovely, sweet scent; lily-whites are tiny and white. Some people consider lotus blossoms sacred, or very special. A *poppet* is a little person or doll.

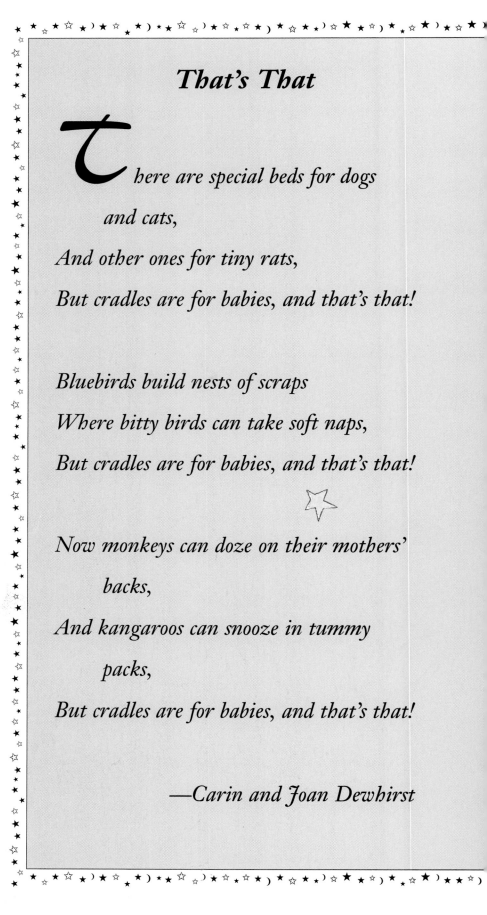

That's That

There are special beds for dogs
*   and cats,*
And other ones for tiny rats,
But cradles are for babies, and that's that!

Bluebirds build nests of scraps
Where bitty birds can take soft naps,
But cradles are for babies, and that's that!

Now monkeys can doze on their mothers'
*   backs,*
And kangaroos can snooze in tummy
*   packs,*
But cradles are for babies, and that's that!

—Carin and Joan Dewhirst

Cradle Song

A cradle is a simple thing—a small bed in which a baby can be rocked to sleep. The first cradle was probably designed so that the mother could easily rock it with her foot. This kept her hands free to knit or spin yarn. Of course she could also sing lullabies while rocking and knitting.

All around the world there are very elaborate cradle customs. For instance, in Ireland the cradle for a first child is always a borrowed one. And did you know that some people believe you should never rock an empty cradle? In Sweden it is believed that this will make a baby extra noisy. In some parts of England they laughingly say you'll have lots and lots of babies if you rock an empty cradle. In most places it's just plain bad luck.

Hush-a-bye, Baby, upon the treetop,

When the wind blows, the cradle will rock;

When the bough breaks the cradle will fall,

Down tumbles Baby and cradle and all.

There are those who believe that babies in cradles need protection from bad fairies, and so some lullabies or cradlesongs are in the form of prayers to good spirits, asking them to guard the baby. (In olden times parents used a magic charm, such as a sprig of mistletoe, to protect a sleeping baby.) An old Scottish lullaby requests angels to "shine over the cradle" and warns bad fairies to "go away far." It is said that a butterfly flitting around a cradle means an angel is passing by, and there are some people who say that a baby who smiles while slumbering is being kissed by an angel.

Even contemporary songs, such as Sandi Patti's "Cradle Song," show how these older customs still influence people's lives. Sandi Patti does not sing about fairies; nonetheless, her song is a plea for protection, although in this case it is a heartfelt prayer to God to hear her concerns for her child.

It is important to note that not all fairies are bad. Good fairies also hover around cradles and safeguard children or help them have sweet dreams. "Queen Mab" is a poem about a good fairy.

Queen Mab

A little fairy comes at night,
Her eyes are blue, her hair is brown,
With silver spots upon her wings,
And from the moon she flutters down.

She has a little silver wand,
And when a good child goes to bed
She waves her hand from right to left,
And makes a circle round its head.

And then it dreams of pleasant things,
Of fountains filled with fairy fish,
And trees that bear delicious fruit,
And bow their branches at a wish;
Of arbors filled with dainty scents
From lovely flowers that never fade;
Bright flies that glitter in the sun,
And glowworms shining in the shade:

And talking birds with gifted tongues,
For singing songs and telling tales,
And pretty dwarfs to show the way
Through fairy hills and fairy dales.

—*Thomas Hood*

When the Day Turns into Night

You can sing a lullaby to anyone or anything—even a favorite pet. Is it time for your cat to go to bed? Is kitty too frisky? Create a kitty lullaby:

Kitty, kitty, far too frisky,

Now is time for bed.

Kitty, kitty, far too

frisky,

On your tail, rest

your head.

Lullabies are songs from the heart, so they can be about happy things, such as love and sunny days, or sad things, such as worries and hurts. Mister Rogers gently tells us in "When the Day Turns into Night" that we can't always be with those who love us, but that even during those "far apart" times loved ones can be together in thought. Saying "good night" and going to sleep can be difficult, but lullabies remind us that love will help us make it through anything—even the darkest night.

All Through the Night

Sleep, my babe, lie still and slumber,

All through the night,

Guardian angels God will lend thee,

All through the night;

Soft, the drowsy hours are creeping,

Hill and vale in slumber steeping,

Mother, dear, her watch is keeping,

All through the night.

—anonymous

Basque Lullaby

*Lullaby, twilight is spreading
Silver wings over the sky;
Fairy elves are softly treading,
Folding buds as they pass by.*

*Lullaby, whisper and sigh
Lullaby, lullaby.*

*Lullaby, deep in the clover
Drones the bee, softly to rest.*

*Close white lids, your dear eyes over,
Mother's arms shall be your nest.*

Lullaby, whisper and sigh
Lullaby, lullaby.

—anonymous

Voyage for Dreamers

It might be difficult, but as you listen to Pamala Ballingham sing "Voyage for Dreamers," close your eyes and imagine a dreamland of your very own. Dreamland is a different place for everyone, but there are those who say that dreamland is definitely somewhere far away, past the sea of stars in the night sky. Look up at the stars one night and perhaps you will see as far as dreamland.

Wynken, Blynken, and Nod

Wynken, Blynken, and Nod
one night
Sailed off in a wooden shoe—
Sailed on a river of crystal light,
Into a sea of dew.
"Where are you going, and what do you
wish?"
The old moon asked the three.
"We have come to fish for the herring fish
That live in this beautiful sea;
Nets of silver and gold have we!"
Said Wynken, Blynken,
And Nod.

The old moon laughed and sang a song,
As they rocked in the wooden shoe,
And the wind that sped them all night long

Ruffled the waves of dew.

The little stars were the herring fish

That lived in that beautiful sea—

"Now cast your nets wherever you wish—

Never afeard are we";

So cried the stars to the fishermen three:

Wynken, Blynken,

And Nod.

All night long their nets they threw

To the stars in the twinkling foam—

Then down from the skies came the

wooden shoe,

Bringing the fishermen home;

'Twas all so pretty a sail it seemed

As if it could not be,

And some folks thought 'twas a dream they'd

dreamed

Of sailing that beautiful sea—

But I shall name you the fishermen three:

Wynken, Blynken,

And Nod.

Wynken and Blynken are two little eyes,

And Nod is a little head,

And the wooden shoe that sailed the skies

Is the wee one's trundle-bed.

So shut your eyes while mother sings

Of wonderful sights that be,

And you shall see the beautiful things

As you rock in the misty sea,

Where the old shoe rocked the fishermen three:

Wynken, Blynken,

And Nod.

—Eugene Field

Goodnight, My Someone

Mr. Meredith Willson wrote "Goodnight, My Someone" for a musical called *The Music Man*. The song is about saying "goodnight" to one you love. But what if you lived in a place where there was no need to say "goodnight"? Where would it be and what would it be like?

Long, long ago and far, far away, at the very top of the world there was a place that had no daylight...a land filled with darkness. Life was hard in this place. People worked at all different times and slept at all different times because they never knew when exactly it was morning and when exactly it was bedtime. It never seemed right to wish anyone "goodnight."

In this faraway place there lived a very sleek, very black crow who looked even blacker and sleeker in all that darkness. Not only was he sleek and black, he also had magic powers. He could fly for very long distances for very long periods of time and he loved to tell very long tales of where he had been and what he had seen. He would fly in and out of people's homes and entertain them with news of the bigger, wider world.

One day (or was it night?) Crow returned after an especially long journey with unusual news. As he flapped from house to house he told the townsfolk about something he had seen that was a shame they didn't have. He called it "daylight."

"So, what is it, this daylight?" one old man asked.

"Well," said Crow speaking in his caw, "daylight is something that makes it possible to really see everything. If you folks up here had some, why, you could go wherever you wanted to and you could see things even when they were very, very far away. It would make your life much easier, yes indeedy, yes indeedy."

"Dear Crow, wise Crow, brave Crow," said the Mayor, "would you consider flying forth and bringing back some of this special daylight that could so dramatically change our lifestyle?"

Crow hesitated and then squawked, "Oh, this place that has daylight is very far away, and besides, how would I carry it back? I might also mention that I would be stealing it as well. No, I think the task is too risky, too risky."

"Oh, dearest Crow, wisest Crow, bravest Crow," crooned the Mayor, "if you bring home the daylight we will award you the highest honors we have ever awarded anyone. We will prepare an enormous feast for you and with our new daylight, everyone will be able to see how very sleek and clever you really are. That's an offer you don't get every day—or night, either."

Well, Crow was finally persuaded to attempt the task. Although he had been to the land of daylight before, he wasn't exactly sure of the route or how long it would take. He flew for miles and miles and miles. It was dark and it was cold. He was very tired but he refused to give up. At last he began to notice that things were getting brighter. He could see shapes a long way off and it seemed to him that all the light was coming from one very large house on the very tip of a mountaintop. The closer he flew, the brighter everything was, and soon he arrived on the front doorstep of that very house. No sooner had he folded his sleek wings behind him than the door opened and he caught a glimpse inside. Daylights were everywhere! There were some very large ones and several very small ones; they were on tables and chairs, stashed on bookshelves, and rolled away in corners. Some looked heavy and some looked light, but none looked easy to carry.

It was going to take a lot of magic to get Crow inside that house. Fortunately, Crow had some stored away for just such an occasion. As he unbuttoned his sleek, black feathered skin and peeled it off, he cawed a powerful charm under his breath.

Long ago and far away I dreamed a dream of yesterday

Tomorrow comes but has no eyes

Today is here but in disguise

Far away and long ago the dream is here and here I go.

Slowly he began to shrink until he was no larger than the dot at the end of this sentence. The next time the door of the house opened, Crow grabbed the first gust of air that came his way and rode right on in. A small child was playing with all sorts of toys in the middle of the room, where Crow landed along with some other bits of

dust. He found himself wedged between two large build-
ing blocks and a big stuffed dog. His eyes began to focus
on a dazzling toy the little boy was dragging around at
the end of a long string. It was a brilliant little daylight
and Crow was nearly blinded as it rolled past him.

Knowing he had not a moment to lose, Crow sum-
moned his feathered suit.

Come along now little skin

Step right up and I'll step in

Inside-out or outside-in

Sure-footed feathers come in, come in.

Quickly Crow wiggled himself into his bodysuit and snatched the string attached to the daylight from the child's fingers. The boy let out a scream just as his father walked through the front door. Crow flew past him with the daylight trailing behind. The father rushed to comfort his crying son; by the time he realized what Crow had done, the bird and the daylight were just a small glow in the distant sky.

The return flight was much easier thanks to the light and the warmth of the daylight. The miles seemed to melt away and soon Crow found himself directly above the Mayor's house. He let the string drop from his beak, and the daylight fell to the ground, where it exploded into a million dazzling pieces.

The townsfolk came rushing out into the street, now totally bathed in daylight, where they began to really see each other for the very first time. The Mayor ordered a

sumptuous banquet to be prepared and everyone ate for hours and hours. Sometime later someone noticed that the daylight was starting to dim.

"Hey, Mr. Crow," shouted a young woman in the crowd, "the daylight you brought us is no good!"

Crow preened his sleek feathers and replied in his proudest caw, "No need to fret. It will continue to get dark regularly, but then just as regularly, the daylight will return. I brought you the finest daylight that exists and it will last as long as the world continues to turn around. The problem was that I could carry only a very small piece of daylight. If I had stolen a large one, it would never have gotten dark here again, no siree, no siree." With that Crow yawned, tucked his head under his sleek wing, and fell fast asleep.

And so the townsfolk wished everyone "goodnight" and went straight to bed.

Where should baby rest?

Where should baby rest?
Where but on its mother's arm—
Where can a baby lie
Half so safe from every harm?
Lulla, lulla, lullaby,
Softly sleep, my baby;
Lulla, lulla, lullaby,
Soft, soft, my baby.

Nestle there, my lovely one!
Press to mine your velvet cheek;
Sweetly coo, and smile, and look
All the love you cannot speak.
Lulla, lulla, lullaby,
Softly sleep, my baby;
Lulla, lulla, lullaby,
Soft, soft, my baby.

—anonymous

Bibliography

Adams, Richard. *The Unbroken Web.* New York: Crown Pub., Inc., 1980.

Daiken, Leslie. *The Lullaby Book.* London: Edmund Ward Pub. LTD, 1959.

Giudice, Luisa Del. "Ninna-nanna-nonsense? Fears, Dreams, and Falling in the Italian Lullaby." *Oral Tradition*, Vol. 3, No. 3 (1988), pp. 270–293.

Gujikawawe, Gyo. *A Child's Book of Poems.* New York: Grosset & Dunlop, 1979.

Hearn, Michael Patrick, ed. *The Victorian Fairy Tale Book.* New York: Pantheon Books, 1988.

Marks, Claude. *Go In and Out the Window.* New York: Henry Holt and Company, 1987.

Wilder, Alec; illustrated by Maurice Sendak. *Lullabies and Night Songs.* New York: Harper and Row, 1965.

Recommended Reading

Brown, Margaret Wise. *Goodnight Moon.* New York: Harper and Row, 1947.

Chorao, Kay. *The Baby's Bedtime Book.* New York: Dutton, 1984.

———. *The Baby's Good Morning Book.* New York: Dutton, 1990.

———. *The Baby's Lap Book.* New York: Dutton, 1990.

———. *The Baby's Story Book.* New York: Dutton, 1989.

———. *The Child's Story Book.* New York: Dutton, 1987.

Hoban, Russell. *Bedtime for Frances.* New York: Harper and Row, 1960.

Mayle, Peter. *Sweet Dreams and Monsters.* New York: Crown Publishing Group, 1986.

Ormerod, Jan. *Moonlight.* New York: Lothrop, 1982.

———. *Sunshine.* New York: Lothrop, 1981.

Rockwell, Anne. *The Three Bears and 15 Other Stories.* New York: Thomas Y. Crowell Company, 1982.

Potter, Beatrix. *Peter Rabbit Collection.* New York: Frederick Warne, 1988.

Rojankovsky, Reodor, illus. *The Tall Book of Nursery Tales.* New York: Harper & Row, 1980.

Rockwell, Anne. *The Three Bears and 15 Other Stories*. New York: Thomas Y. Crowell Company, 1982.

Rojankovsky, Reodor, illus. *The Tall Book of Nursery Tales*. New York: Harper & Row, 1980.

Sendak, Maurice. *Where the Wild Things Are*. New York: Harper and Row, 1963.

Yolen, Jane. *The Lullaby Songbook*. San Diego: Harcourt Brace, 1986.

—————. *Owl Moon*. New York: Philomel, 1987.

Recommended Listening

A Child's Gift of Lullabies. JABA Records, 1987 (also available in Spanish).

Herdman, Priscilla. *Star Dreamer*. Alacazam! Records, 1988.

Lee, Robert. *Sound-a-Sleep*. Robert D. Lee Music, 1984.

Lullabies for Little Dreamers. CMS Records, Inc., 1987.

Lullabies Go Jazz. Arranged and produced by Jon Crosse for Jazz Cat Productions, 1985.

Lullaby Magic. Discovery Magic, 1985.

'Til Their Eyes Shine (The Lullaby Album). Columbia Records, 1992.

Wilder, Alec. *Lullabies and Night Songs*. Caedmon, 1985.

The World Sings Goodnight. Silver Wave Records, 1993.

Index